Anonymous

**Choosing**

Anonymous

**Choosing**

ISBN/EAN: 9783337196974

Printed in Europe, USA, Canada, Australia, Japan

Cover: Foto ©Andreas Hilbeck / pixelio.de

More available books at **www.hansebooks.com**

# CHOOSING
# "ABE" LINCOLN
# CAPTAIN

*AND*
*OTHER*
*STORIES*

Illustrated

The Werner Company

NEW YORK     AKRON, OHIO     CHICAGO

1899

"O, THE DEAR ONES AT HOME!"

# CHOOSING "ABE" CAPTAIN.

WHEN the Black Hawk war broke out in Illinois about 1832, young Abraham Lincoln was living at New Salem, a little village of the class familiarly known at the west as "one-horse towns," and located near the capital city of Illinois.

He had just closed his clerkship of a year in a feeble grocery, and was the first to enlist under the call of Governor Reynolds for volunteer forces to go against the Sacs and Foxes, of whom Black Hawk was chief.

By treaty these Indians had been removed west of the Mississippi into Iowa; but, thinking their old hunting-grounds the better, they had recrossed the river with their war-paint on, causing some trouble, and a great deal of alarm among the settlers. Such was the origin of the war; and the handful of government troops stationed at Rock Island wanted help. Hence the State call.

Mr. Lincoln was twenty-three years old at that time, nine years older than his adopted state. The country was thinly settled, and a company of ninety men who could be spared from home for military service had to be gathered from a wide district. When full, the company met at the neighboring village of Richland to choose its officers. In those days the militia men were allowed to select their leaders in their own way ; and they had a very peculiar mode of expressing their preference for captains. For then, as now, there were almost always two candidates for one office.

They would meet on the green somewhere, and at the appointed hour, the competitors would step out from the crowds on the opposite sides of the ground, and each would call on all the "boys" who wanted him for captain to fall in behind him. As the line formed, the man next the candidate would put his hands on the candidate's shoulder ; the third man also in the same manner to the second man ; and so on to the end. And then they would march and cheer for their leader like so many wild men, in order to win over the fellows who didn't seem to have a choice, or whose minds were sure to run after the greater noise. When all had taken sides, the man who led the longer line, would be declared captain

Mr Lincoln never outgrew the familiar nickname, "Abe," but at that time he could hardly be said to have any other name than " Abe ;" in fact he had emerged from clerking in that little corner grocery as "Honest Abe." He was not only liked, but loved, in the rough fashion of the frontier by all who knew him. He was a good hand at gunning, fishing, racing, wrestling and other games ; he had a tall and strong figure ; and he seemed to have been as often "reminded of a little story " in '32 as in '62. And the few men not won by these qualities, were won and held by his great common sense, which restrained him from excesses even in sports, and made him a safe friend.

It is not singular therefore that though a stranger to many of the enlisted men, he should have had his warm friends who at once determined to make him captain.

But Mr. Lincoln hung back with the feeling, he said, that if there was any older and better established citizen whom the " boys " had confidence in, it would be better to make such a one captain. His poverty was even more marked than his modesty ;

and for his stock in education about that time, he wrote in a letter to a friend twenty-seven years, later:

"I did not know much; still, somehow, I could read, write, and cipher to the rule of three, but that was all."

That, however, was up to the average education of the community; and having been clerk in a country grocery he was considered an educated man.

In the company Mr. Lincoln had joined, there was a dapper little chap for whom Mr. Lincoln had labored as a farm hand a year before, and whom he had left on account of ill treatment from him. This man was eager for the captaincy. He put in his days and nights "log-rolling" among his fellow volunteers; said he had already smelt gunpowder in a brush with Indians, thus urging the value of experience; even thought he had a "martial bearing;" and he was very industrious in getting those men to join the company who would probably vote for him to be captain.

Muster-day came, and the recruits met to organize. About them stood several hundred relatives and other friends.

The little candidate was early on hand and busily bidding for votes. He had felt so confident of the office in advance of muster-day, that he had rummaged through several country tailor-shops and got a new suit of the nearest approach to a captain's uniform that their scant stock could furnish. So there he was, arrayed in jaunty cap, and a swallow-tailed coat with brass buttons. He even wore fine boots, and moreover *had them blacked* — which was almost a crime among a country crowd of that day.

Young Lincoln took not one step to make himself captain ; and not one to prevent it. He simply put himself "in the hands of his friends," as the politicians say. He stood and quietly watched the trouble others were borrowing over the matter as if it were an election of officers they had enlisted for, rather than for fighting Indians. But after all a good deal depends in war, on getting good officers.

As two o'clock drew near, the hour set for making captain, four or five of young Lincoln's most zealous friends with a big stalwart fellow at the head edged along pretty close to him, yet not in a way to excite suspicion of a "conspiracy." Just a little bit before two, without even letting "Abe" himself know exactly "what was up," the big fellow stepped directly behind him, clapped his hands on the shoulders before him, and shouted as only prairie giants can, "Hurrah for Captain Abe Lincoln ! " and plunged his really astonished candidate forward into a march.

At the same instant, those in league with him also put hands to the shoulders before them, pushed, and took up the cheer, " Hurrah for Captain Abe Lincoln ! " so loudly that there seemed to be several hundred already on their side ; and so there were, for the outside crowd was also already cheering for " Abe."

This little " ruse " of the Lincoln " boys " proved a complete success. " Abe" had to march, whether or no, to the music of their cheers ; he was truly " in the hands of his friends " then, and couldn't get away ; and it must be said he didn't seem to feel very bad over the situation. The storm of cheers and the sight of tall Abraham (six feet and four inches) at the head of the marching column, before the fussy little chap in brass buttons was quite ready, caused a quick stampede even among the boys who intended to vote for the little fellow. One after another they rushed for a place in " Captain Abe's " line as though to be first to fall in was to win a prize.

A few rods away stood that suit of captain's clothes alone, looking smaller than ever, " the starch all taken out of 'em," their occupant confounded, and themselves for sale. " Abe's " old " boss " said he was " astonished," and so he had good reason to be, but everybody could see it without his saying so. His "style" couldn't win among the true and shrewd, though unpolished " boys " in coarse garments. They saw right through him.

" Buttons," as he became known from that day, was the last man to fall into " Abe's" line ; he said he'd make it unanimous.

But his experience in making " Abe " Captain made himself so sick that he wasn't " able " to move when the company left for the " front," though he soon grew able to move out of the procession.

Thus was " Father Abraham," so young as twenty three, chosen captain of a militia company over him whose abused, hired-hand he had been. It is little wonder that in '59 after three elections to the State Legislature and one to Congress, Mr. Lincoln should write of this early event as " a success which gave me more pleasure than any I have had since." Tne war was soon over with but little field work for the volunteers ; but no private was known to complain that " Abe " was not a good captain.

# SALLY'S SEVEN-LEAGUE SHOES.

D ID you never hear the story of Sally Colman's shoes?

Why, they went far ahead of Jack's seven-league boots! They walked all the way from Hatfield, Massachusetts, to Canada and back, walking straight over Lake Champlain without sinking — they were bound with silk from Paris and threaded with deer's sinew from the forest, and soled with leather from England, and the red serge uppers came by way of New Amsterdam, straight from Holland, and with all the rough usage to which they were put they have lasted two hundred years and are not quite worn out yet; indeed it is very possible that they may last twice two hundred years longer. Now, is not that wonderful? And the most wonderful thing about the story is — that it is quite true.

One bright morning early in September, 1677, little
Sally Colman sat on the counter of the Hatfield store
swinging her feet complacently, and not a little proud
of the new pair of red shoes which the shopkeeper
had just fitted to them. She was on the point of
jumping down and running home, when Mistress Delight Crowninshield, a young lady of great consequence from Boston, who had been visiting relatives
in Hatfield that summer, inquired of the shopkeeper,
who was also the postmaster, for her mail. Little
Sally Colman watched her with great awe, as she re-
ceived from deferential hands a brown paper parcel
heavily besplashed with huge red seals.

"They are my slippers!" exclaimed Mistress Delight in a tone of vexation, as she tore open the parcel, "and just too late for the husking frolic at Benoni Stebbins' barn!"

She placed the dainty slippers on the counter and
looked at them regretfully; and Sally, as her round,
young eyes noted their French heels and the delicate
roseate hue of the silk, with the sparkle of the small
paste-buckles on the instep, thought she had never
seen anything half so lovely in all her short life, and
looked down with diminished pride at her own heel-
less, stout-soled little boots with their red serge
uppers and waxed-end ties.

"After all," sighed Mistress Crowninshield, "perhaps it is quite for the best. I should certainly have split them dancing, 'I'll be married in my old clothes,' on that rough plank floor, and now I shall have them fresh for Boston, for I am going back to-morrow, and who knows what flowery paths they may lead me in? Good bye, little Sally — so you have a pair of new shoes, too! Almost as big as mine, as stout and strong as you are, and as red as your own cheeks, while mine are only bits of silken flimsiness like myself. Their histories, if anybody could write them, will doubtless be much like our own lives. Yours will probably last long and finally be stubbed out among the huckleberries and the dandelions, and mine will grow faded and shabby to the squeak of fiddlers and the glare of sconces, and they will both be buried in Nature's rag-bag and be alike forgotten."

Goodman Plympton, who liked to listen to Mistress Delight's playful chatter, shook his head gravely at this speech.

"Nay, Mistress Crowninshield," he said, "I have known the most humble raiment to be treasured carefully from generation to generation, long after the whilom owners thereof had perished, in memory of some noble deed which they had done in their lifetime, and which forbade that they should ever be forgotten."

"We have my grandfather's soiled gauntlets, for he fought with Cromwell," said Mistress Delight.

MISTRESS DELIGHT MORALIZES.

"And mother has wrapped in fine white paper the sprigged veil which my grandmother made and wore," said little Sally.

"Yea," replied Goodman Plimpton, "your grandmother was a French Huguenot. The veil is but a bit of silken flimsiness, of a piece with your slippers, Mistress Delight, but it has endured, for it holds within it something of the grace and loveliness of the wearer and maker, for it is written that though all things else vanish away, yet love abideth. And the gloves of your grandfather, though rough and uncomely, yet speak a stout heart and noble deeds, and these cannot die, fair Mistress Delight."

Delight Crowninshield went to Boston, and the peach-blossom tinted slippers graced her feet at all of the few merry-makings in which the prim little town indulged. At one of these she met a young Frenchman from Quebec, an officer under the great Count Fontenac, who was in Boston on business of his command. This officer thought he had never seen anyone as beautiful as Delight Crowinshield, and during his stay in Boston he was constantly at her side.

One day as they were walking in Frog Lane, now Boylston street, Delight found that she had lost one of her paste shoe-buckles, and that she would soon lose the slipper also, if it were not replaced.

They stepped into a shop, and the Frenchman bought a buckle and, dropping on one knee, placed Delight's little foot on the other while he fastened the slipper snugly for her. But Boston mud in Frog Lane then was quite as bad as Boston mud in Boyl-

ston street now, and when Delight removed her foot
the print of her sole was startlingly visible on the
French officer's fine white broadcloth knee-breeches.

IN FROG LANE, BOSTON.

"I fear me it will not come off," said Delight, rue-
fully.

"Then let it remain," replied the gallant Frenchman. "I shall guard it as the proudest decoration I
possess until the day that I can claim little foot and
little body as my own."

Wooings were rather more stately and lengthy things

in those days than now, and the French officer was
obliged to go back to Quebec wearing a new pair of
knee-breeches, the stained ones folded away in his
chest, and only the vague assurance that he might
claim Mistress Delight as his bride when it was
plainly proved that he deserved her.

He had scarcely gone when very sorrowful news
was heard from Hatfield. The Indians had made a
descent upon the town, had burned, and pillaged, and
murdered, and carried away captive. Little Sally
Colman's mother was killed and Sally herself carried
to Canada.

Poor little Sally! She had been rudely waked up
that chill autumn morning by glare of fire and shrieks
and horrid yells, but as she was dragged out of the
burning house she caught at the objects dearest to
her heart — her new red shoes. Many a weary mile
the little captive trudged meekly, uncomplainingly,
until the heart of even her Indian captor was touched,
and he lifted her to his shoulders as they strode
through the thick underbrush.

Often the straggling band would be separated, and
then they kept near each other by uttering hideous
noises; hooting like screech-owls, or howling like
wolves. When Sally heard these sounds she would
start with fright, and cling to Painted Arrow's neck;

ALL THE WAY TO CANADA.

until the savage, seeing how she trusted in him for protection, answered her confidence with every kindness in his power to grant.

When they climbed the steep mountains he placed her on one of the horses behind one of the two ugly-faced squaws who accompanied the party, and when she trembled with the quivering of the frail birch-bark canoe, in which they crossed the Connecticut, he leaped into the deadly-cold water and followed her, swimming by its side and steadying it now and then with his hand.

They crossed the river several times, keeping it between them and the English settlements as they travelled northward. The Indians hunted as they went, and Painted Arrow always shared his portion with little Sally, who learned to consider a roasted bear's paw a great delicacy. Once they had huckleberries which the squaws gathered ; but in getting them the squaws lost Benoni Stebbins, whom they had taken with them to carry the full baskets, and Benoni, making his way back to Hatfield, told their friends at home of their sufferings and put stout-hearted pursuers upon their track.

The Indians toiled over the Green Mountains and reached Lake Champlain only to find it frozen. Here they made sledges, and Painted Arrow placed Sally and little Samuel Russell, who had been taken captive at Deerfield, on one of these and tucking them in with skins and his own blanket drew them over the ice. But in spite of his care the boy died, and when they reached Chamblee some of the more cruel Indians burned Goodman Plympton at the stake.

It was Christmas time when they reached Sorel, a French garrison on the St. Lawrence river, and here Sally and the other captives were sold as slaves to the French settlers. The French masters were kinder to them than their Indian ones had been, and Sally attended the Christmas service at the little Jesuit church, thankful at heart that the perilous journey was accomplished.

After service there was a Christmas dinner such as Sally had never tasted, for her master, Jean Poitevin, had been a prince of cooks in his native land, and he donned a white apron and paper cap and served up a dinner that would have done honor to a Parisian restaurant. In the first place there was a delicious soup made of the legs and head of a rooster, an onion, a carrot cut in fancy pieces, a bouquet of different kinds of herbs, and a piece of garlic. Then there was *gibelotte de lapin*, a rabbit stewed in a delicious black sauce. This was accompanied by blocks of bread cut from a loaf about as long as Jean Poitevin's arm.

23

Next came the rooster served with little mushrooms all around him, big ones tucked under his wings and a button-hole knot of them on his breast. After this Sally helped Madame Poitevin to clear away the meats, and the family attacked the dessert which had all along ornamented the central part of the table, and consisted of a temple of macaroons marvellously iced and decorated, six little pots of six different kinds of preserves, and some very black coffee.

Poor little Sally ! The kindness of her new owners was quite as bad for her as the severity of the Indians, and the varied bill of fare, after her scanty diet of bear's-paws and acorns, made her very ill. Madame Poitevin nursed her very kindly, and mended her little red shoes, which had become very ragged with the long march. The Indians had replaced the shoestrings by deer-sinews, and Madame Poitevin bound the worn edge with a ribbon which she had brought with her from France. Then she took out her lace pillow, and Sally, as she watched the growth of the frost-like sprays, thought of her grandmother's sprigged veil which lasted so long, and of Goodman Plympton's words — " Love endureth." By her loving ways and gentle, obedient behavior she won the Poitevins' hearts ; but in spite of their kindness the tears would often well to her eyes, and she would sob :

"Father, father, shall I ever see you and dear old Hatfield again ? "

And ever since the return of Benoni Stebbins, Sally's father and the good Hatfield people generally had been doing their best for the rescue of their kidnapped neighbors.  Benjamin Wait and Stephen Jennings, whose wives had been carried away, were most forward of all.  They went to Albany and tried to obtain soldiers to follow the Indians.  But instead of being helped they were hindered, for the Dutch and Yankees were not very friendly at this time, and they were thrown into prison for a while, so that it was not until December that these two brave men, with only a friendly Mohawk Indian for a guide, set out for Canada.

When Delight Crowninshield heard of this expedition it struck her that perhaps she could do something to help it along, and seizing her father's stubby goose-quill, she wrote the following quaint letter to the French officer who had carried away the print of her small foot on his knee and heart:

RESP'D SIR : There has been an incursion of ye barbarous savages who have captivated many of ye people of Hatfield leading them away to Canada.  Certain of our people, Benjamin

Wait and Stephen Jenning, are now on their way to Quebec to obtain the deliverance of the same, which if thou canst effect or aid through thy influence with thy master, the great Governor Fontinac, thou mayest make any demand upon my kindness which thou seest fit. In witness whereof I hereto set my hand and seal this 15th day of November, 1676.

DELIGHT CROWNINSHIELD.

The seal which the little witch affixed was two drops of black sealing wax, artfully managed to resemble the print of a slipper.

This was enough. When the Hatfield ambassadors reached Quebec they were brought at once before Fontinac, and the release of all the captives ordered. A guard of French soldiers was also granted to convey them safely to Hatfield.

They set out on their homeward journey the middle of April and arrived in the early summer, little Sally still wearing the remnants of her seven-league shoes — two very worn soles with little of the scarlet uppers and a frayed morsel of French ribbon left, each clinging to the ankle only by a string of stout deer's sinew.

The young French officer, who you may be sure formed one of the guard, quickly made an exchange of prisoners, for though he returned Sally to her home, he carried Delight back with him to Quebec in a far more "captivated" condition than any of the

prisoners taken by the Indians. And Madame Delight's first wifely duty was to scour long and ear-
nestly a spot of Boston mud left on a pair of her
husband's white knee-breeches. But the mud had
been left untouched so long that it never thoroughly
came out; and the gallant French officer told the
story of the half effaced footprint many times amidst

the applause of his comrades and even of Count
Fontenac himself.

You can see one of Sally's red shoes to-day in the
museum of the Memorial Association at Deerfield —
the little shoe that trudged to Canada and back, and
has lasted, unlike most children's shoes, over two hundred years. The other is in the collection at the Old
South Church in Boston, and was referred to in the
WIDE AWAKE for July, 1879, in an article entitled
" The Children's Hour at the Old South."

That "Love endureth," though slipper-prints fade and shoes wear out, and that patient submission will conquer in the end, is the lesson of Sally's little shoes.

# THE LOST DIAMOND SNUFF BOX.

THE grand old kingdom of England, in the course of the mossy centuries you can count over its head, has had its times of gloom and depression at dangers that looked near, and its times of shouting and rejoicing over dangers its brave men have driven away quite out of sight again.

One of the deepest seasons of gloom was when the French Emperor, Napoleon, had conquered one country after another, until there was scarcely anything but England left to attack ; and one of the proudest times of rejoicing was when the " Iron Duke " Wellington, and the bluff old Prussian, Blücher, met him at Waterloo, defeated his armies and drove him from the field. There were bonfires, and bell-ringings then, and from that day onward England loved and cherished every man who had fought at Waterloo —

from the Iron Duke himself down to the plainest private, every one was a hero and a veteran.

In one of the humblest houses of a proud nobleman's estate, a low, whitewashed cottage, one of these veterans lived not so very many years ago. He had fought by his flag in one of the most gallant regiments until the last hour of the battle, and then had fallen disabled from active service for the rest of his life.

That did not seem to be of so very great consequence, though, just now; for peace reigned in the land, and with his wife and two beautiful daughters to love, his battles to think over, and his pension to provide the bread and coffee, the old soldier was as happy as the day was long. It made no difference that the bread and the coffee were both black, and the clothes of the veteran were coarse and seldom new.

" Ho, Peggy ! " he used to say to his wife, " my cloak is as fine as the one the Iron Duke wore when they carried me past him just as the French were breaking; and as for the bread, only a veteran knows how the recollection of victory makes everything taste sweet ! "

But it seemed as if the old soldier's life was going to prove like his share in that great day at Waterloo

— success and victory till the end had nearly come, and then one shot after another striking him with troubles he could never get over.

The first came in the midst of the beautiful summer days, when the bees droned through the delicious air, the rose-bush was in full bloom, and the old soldier sat in the cottage door revelling in it all. A slow, merciless fever rose up through the soft air — it did not venture near the high ground where the castle stood, but it crept noiselessly into the whitewashed cottage, one night, and the soldier's two daughters were stricken down. This was the beginning of terrible trouble to the veteran of Waterloo. Not that he minded watching, for he was used to standing sentry all night, and as for nursing, he had seen plenty of the hospital ; but to see his daughters suffering — that was what he could not bear !

And worst of all, between medicines and necessaries for the sick, the three months' pension was quite used up, and when the old soldier's nursing had pulled through the fierceness of the fever, there was nothing but black bread left in the house — and black bread was almost the same as no bread at all to the dainty appetites the fever had left ; and that was what he had to think of, and think of, as he sat in the cottage door.

" Bah ! " said the old soldier, with something more

like a groan than was ever heard from him while his wounds were being dressed, " I could face all the ar mies of Napoleon better than this ! "

And he sat more and more in the cottage door, as if that could leave the trouble behind ; but it stood staring before him, all the same, till it almost shut the rosebush and the bees out of sight. But one morning a tremendous surprise came to him like a flash out of the sky ! He heard the sound of galloping troops, and he pricked up his ears, for that always made him think of a cavalry charge.

" Who goes there ? " he cried ; but without answering his challenge the sound came nearer and nearer, and a lackey in full livery dashed up to the door, and presented him with a note sealed with the blood-red seal of the castle arms. It was an invitation to dine at the castle with a company of noblemen and officers of the army. His lordship, who had also fought at Waterloo, had just learned that a comrade was living on his estate, and made haste to do him honor, and secure a famous guest for his dinner party.

The old soldier rose up proudly, and gave the lackey a military salute.

" Tell his lordship," he said, " that I shall report myself at head-quarters, and present my thanks for the honor he has done me."

The lackey galloped off, and the veteran pushed his chair over with his wooden leg, and clattered across the cottage floor.

"Ho, Peggy!" he cried, "did I not say that luck comes and trouble flies if you only face the enemy long enough? This is the beginning of good things, I tell you! A hero of Waterloo, and fit to dine with lords and generals, will certainly have other good fortune coming to him, till he can keep his wife and daughters like princesses. Just wait a bit and you shall see!" and he turned hastily away, for his heart came up in his throat so that he could not speak.

All the rest of that day he sat in the door, brushing and darning and polishing his stained uniform. It had lain abandoned on the shelf for many a year, but before night every button was shining like gold, the scarlet cloth was almost fresh once more, and the old soldier, wrapped in his faithful cloak, was making his way joyfully across the heathery moors to the castle quite at the other side.

But when he had fairly reached it, and the servant had shown him into the drawing-room, his heart almost failed him for a moment. Such splendor he had never seen before — a thousandth part would have bought health and happiness for the dear ones he had left with only his brave goodbye and a fresh rose-bud to comfort them!

However, what with the beautiful ladies of the castle gathering round him to ask questions about the battle, and with a seat near his lordship's right hand at dinner, he soon plucked up again, and began to realize how delightful everything was. But that was the very thing that almost spoiled the whole again, for when he saw his plate covered with luxuries and delicacies more than he could possibly eat, the thought of the black bread he had left at the cottage brought the tears rushing to his eyes.

But, " Tut! " he said to himself in great dismay, " what an ungrateful poltroon his lordship will think he has brought here! " and he managed to brush them off while no one was looking.

It was delicious, though, in spite of everything, and after a while the wine began to flow — that warmed his very heart — and then he heard his lordship calling to a servant to bring him something from his private desk, saying:

"Gentlemen, I am about to show you the proudest treasure I possess. This diamond snuff-box was presented to me by the stout old Blücher himself, in remembrance of service I was able to perform at Waterloo. Not that I was a whit worthier of it than

the brave fellows under my command — understand
that ! "

How the diamonds glistened and gleamed as the
box was passed from hand to hand ! As if the thick-
est cluster of stars you ever saw, could shine out in
the midst of a yellow sunset sky, and the colors of
the rainbow could twinkle through them at the same
time ! It was superb, but then that was nothing com-
pared to the glory of receiving it from Blücher !

Then there was more wine and story-telling, and at
last some one asked to look at the snuff-box again.

" Has any one the snuff-box at present ? " asked
his lordship, rather anxiously, for as he turned to
reach it no snuff-box was to be seen.

No one said " yes," for everyone was sure he had
passed it to his neighbor, and they searched up and
down the table with consternation in their faces, for
the snuff-box could not have disappeared without
hands, but to say so was to touch the honor of gentlemen and soldiers.

At last one of the most famous officers rose from
his seat :

" My lord, he said, " a very unlucky accident
must have occurred here. Some one of us must have
slipped the box into his pocket unconsciously, mis-
taking it for his own. I will take the lead in search-

ing mine, if the rest of the company will follow!"

"Agreed!" said the rest, and each guest in turn went to the bottom of one pocket after another, but still no snuff-box, and the distress of the company increased. The old soldier's turn came last, and with it came the surprise. With burning cheeks and arms folded closely across his breast he stood up and confronted the company like a stag at bay.

"No!" he exclaimed, "no one shall search my pockets! Would you doubt the honor of a soldier?"

"But we have all done so," said the rest, "and every one knows it is the merest accident at the most." But the old soldier only held his arms the tighter, while the color grew deeper in his face. In his perplexity his lordship thought of another expedient.

"We will try another way, gentlemen," he said, "I will order a basket of bran to be brought, and propose that each one in turn shall thrust his hand into the bran. No one shall look on, and if we find the box at last, no one can guess whose hand placed it there."

It was quickly done, and hand after hand was thrust in, until at last came the old soldier's turn once more. But he was no where to be seen.

Then, at last the indignation of the company broke forth.

"A soldier, and a hero of Waterloo, and willing to be a thief!" and with their distress about the affair, and his lordship's grief at his loss, the evening was entirely spoiled.

Meantime the old soldier, with his faithful cloak wrapped closely round him once more, was fighting his way through the sharp winds and over the moors again. But a battle against something a thousand times sharper and colder was going on in his breast.

"A thief!" he was saying over and over to himself, "me, who fought close to the side of the Iron Duke! And yet, can I look one of them in the face and tell him he lies?"

The walk that had been gone over so merrily was a terrible one to retrace, and when the cottage was reached, instead of the pride and good luck the poor invalids had been watching for, a gloom deadlier than the fever followed him in. He sat in the doorway as he used, but sometimes he hung his head on his breast, and sometimes started up and walked proudly about, crying —

"Peggy! I say no one shall call me a thief! I am a soldier of the Iron Duke!"

But they did call him a thief, though, for a very

strange thing, after his lordship had sorrowfully ordered the cottage and little garden spot to be searched no box was found, and the gloom and the mystery grew deeper together.

Good nursing could not balance against trouble like this; the beautiful daughters faded and died, the house was too gloomy to stay inside, and if he escaped to the door, he had to hear the passers say —

"There sits the soldier who stole the Blücher diamonds from his host!"

And as if this was not enough, one day the sound of hoofs was heard again, and a rider in uniform clattered up to the door saying:

"Comrade, I am sent to tell you that your pension is stopped! His Majesty cannot count a thief any longer a soldier of his!"

After this the old soldier hardly held up his head at all, and his hair, that had kept black as a coal all these years, turned white as the moors when the winter snows lay on them.

"Though that is all the same, Peggy," he used to say, "for it is winter all the year round with me! If I could only die as the old year does! That would be the thing!"

But long and merciless as the winter is, spring does

come at last, if we can but live and fight our way through the storms and cold.

One night a cry of fire roused all the country-side. All but the old soldier. He heard them say the castle was burning, but what was that to him? Nothing could burn away the remembrance that he had once been called a thief within its walls! But the next morning he heard a step — not a horse's hoof this time, but a strong man walking hastily towards him.

"Where is the veteran of Waterloo?" asked his lordship's voice, and when the old soldier stepped forward, he threw his arms about his neck with tears and sobs.

"Comrade," he said, "come up to the castle! The snuff-box is found, and I want you to stand in the very room where it was lost while I tell everyone what a great and sorrowful wrong a brave and honest soldier has suffered at my hands!"

It did not take many words to explain. In the first alarm of fire the butler had rushed to the plate-closet to save the silver.

"Those goblets from the high shelf! Quick!" he said, to the footman who was helping him, and with the haste about the goblets something else came tumbling down.

"The lost diamond snuff-box!" cried the butler.

"That stupid fellow I dismissed the day it disappeared, must have put it there and forgotten all about it!"

The fire was soon extinguished, but not a wink of sleep could his lordship get until he could make reparation for the pitiful mistake about the box ; and once more the old soldier made his way across the moors, even the wooden leg stepping proudly as he went along, though now and then, as the old feeling came over him, his white head would droop for a moment again.

The servants stood aside respectfully as he entered the castle, and they and the other guests of that unlucky day gathered round him while his lordship told them how the box had been found and how he could not rest until forgiven by the brave hero he had so unjustly suspected of wrong.

"And now," said the company, "will you not tell us one thing more ? Why did you refuse to empty your pockets, as all the rest were willing to do ? "

"Because," said the old soldier sorrowfully, "because I *was* a thief, and I could not bear that anyone should discover it ! All whom I loved best in the world were lying sick at home, starving for want of the delicacies I could not provide, and I felt as if my heart would break to see my plate heaped with luxu-

ries while they had not so much as a taste! I thought
a mouthful of what I did not need might save them,
and when no one was looking I slipped some choice
bits from my plate between two pieces of bread and
made way with them into my pocket. I could not let
them be discovered for a soldier is too proud to beg,
but oh, my lord, he can bear being called a thief all
his life better than he can dine sumptuously while
there is only black bread at home for the sick and
weak whom he loves!"

Tears came streaming from the old soldier's listen-
ers by this time, and each vied with the other in heap-
ing honors and gifts in place of the disgrace suffered
so long; but all that was powerless to make up for
the past.

Two good lessons may be learned from the story:
Never believe any one guilty who is not really proved
to be so. Never let false shame keep you from
confessing the truth, whether trifling or of importance.

# THE WERNER COMPANY'S PUBLICATIONS.

## THE STORY OF CUBA.

From first to last. By MURAT HALSTEAD, veteran journalist, distinguished war correspondent, brilliant writer; for many years the friend and associate of the "Makers of History" of the Western World. There is no more graphic, incisive writer than he; no shrewder observer of men and events; no one who foretells more unerringly the trend of affairs, their sequence and conclusion. Cuba's struggles for liberty. Cause, crisis and destiny. Elegant silk-finished cloth, emblematic, ink and gold design, plain edges, $2.00; half morocco, corners tipped, gold back and center stamp, marbled edges, $2.75.

## GERMANIA.

Two thousand years of German life. By JOHANNES SCHERR. Three hundred engravings. Text in German only. This famous work by the ablest of modern German historians, is a graphic narrative of the origin and grand career of the German people, a history of their religious, social, and domestic life; their development in literature, science, music, and art, and their advancement in military and political power to their present position as arbiters of the destiny of Europe. Cloth binding, ornamented in black and silver. Price. $1.00.

## THE PRESIDENTIAL COOK BOOK.

The best household compendium published. Has a reputation that is national. It is based on its real worth. Every recipe it contains was actually tested by the authors and found to be invariably successful. Thoroughly up-to-date; large type; large pages plainly indexed. A handy volume. In brief, a perfect cook book. Price, 50 cents.

## JOHN SHERMAN'S RECOLLECTIONS OF FORTY YEARS IN THE HOUSE, SENATE AND CABINET.

An autobiography. Being the personal reminiscences of the author, including the political and financial history of the United States during his public career. The Library Edition is issued in two royal octavo volumes containing over 1,200 pages, bound in the following styles:

Fine English Cloth, gold side and back stamps, plain edges, $7.50 per set.

Full sheep, library style, marbled edges, $10.00 per set.

Half morocco, gold center back, gilt edges, $12.00 per set.

Full Turkey morocco, antique, gilt edges, $16.00 per set.

Autograph edition, limited to one thousand numbered copies, printed on specially made paper, bound in three-quarters calf, gilt top and rough edges, imperial 8vo., boxed, $25.00 per set.

The household edition is issued in one royal octavo volume, containing about 950 pages, printed from new electrotype plates on superfine book paper, richly illustrated with carefully selected views, including places and scenes relating to the author's boyhood; also many portraits of his contemporaries in the Cabinet and Senate. In addition there are a large number of fac simile reproductions of letters from presidents, senators, governors, and well-known private citizens.

Half morocco, gold center back, marbled edges, $6.00.

Cloth, gold side and back stamp, $4.00.

## MILITARY CAREER OF NAPOLEON THE GREAT.

By MONTGOMERY B. GIBBS. Not a technical military history, but a gossipy, anecdotal account of the career of Napoleon Bonaparte as his marshals and generals knew him on the battlefield and around the camp-fire. Crown, 8vo., with 32 full page illustrations. Nearly 600 pages; half green leather; gilt top and back; English laid paper; uncut edges. Price, $1.25.

*For sale by all booksellers, or sent postpaid on receipt of the advertised price.*

## THE WERNER COMPANY, Publishers, - Akron, O.

# THE WERNER COMPANY'S PUBLICATIONS.

## SCENIC AMERICA.

Or the Beauties of the Western Hemisphere. 256 half-tone pictures, with descriptions by JOHN L. STODDARD. Size, 11x14 inches, 128 pages. Bound in cloth with handsome side stamp. Price, 75 cents.

## PERSONAL RECOLLECTIONS OF GENERAL NELSON A. MILES.

The wonderful career of a self-made man. How he rose from a Second Lieutenant to the rank of Commander in Chief of the United States Army. Embracing the thrilling story of his famous Indian campaigns. In this volume the reader is brought face to face with the great Indian leaders : Geronimo, Crazy Horse, Sitting Bull, Chief Joseph, Lame Deer, etc. One of the most remarkable books of the century. A massive volume of 600 pages, printed on fine super-calendered paper, with nearly 200 superb engravings. Illustrated by FREDERIC REMINGTON and other eminent artists. Every page bristles with interest. An ever-changing panorama. A history in itself, distinctive, thrilling and well nigh incredible. Artistic cloth, chaste and elegant design, plain edges, **$4.00**.

## THE THEORY AND PRACTICE OF TEACHING.

Presents the complete writings of DAVID P. PAGE, edited by Supt. J. M. GREENWOOD, of the Kansas City Schools, assisted by Prof. CYRUS W. HODGIN, of Earlham College, Ind. This new, revised and enlarged edition of this marvelously popular work contains a fresh and exceedingly interesting life of its noted author, with portrait. 12mo., 343 pages, cloth binding. Price, **$1.50**.

## THE TEACHER IN LITERATURE.

Revised edition, is a publication of exceptional merit, containing selections from Ascham, Rousseau, Shenstone, Pestalozzi, Cowper, Goethe, Irving, Mitford, Bronte, Thackeray, Dickens, and others who have written on subjects pertaining to educational work from the Elizabethan period down. To this edition Dr. B. A. Hindsdale, Professor of Pedagogy, University of Michigan, has added an exhaustive paper on the history of the schoolmaster from earliest times as he appears in literature. 12mo. 447 pages. Price, **$1.50**.

## MAGNER'S STANDARD HORSE AND STOCK BOOK.

A complete pictorial encyclopedia of practical reference for horse and stock owners. By D. MAGNER, author of the Art of Taming and Training Horses, assisted by twelve leading veterinary surgeons. Comprising over 1,200 pages. Containing over 1,750 illustrations. The finest and most valuable farmer's book in the world. Cloth binding, **$4.00**; half Russia, **$5.50**.

## MARTIAL RECITATIONS.

Collected by JAS. HENRY BROWNLEE. A timely book. Martial recitations, heroic, pathetic, humorous. The rarest gems of patriotic prose and poetry. Non-sectional, enthusing. 12mo; 232 pages ; large, sharp type ; excellent paper ; silk cloth binding, gay and attractive. Price, **$1.00**; the same in handsome paper binding, **50** cents.

## PRACTICAL LESSONS IN SCIENCE.

By Dr. J. T. SCOVELL, for ten years Professor of Natural Science in the Indiana State Normal School. Price, **$1.50**.

## WOMAN, HER HOME, HEALTH AND BEAUTY.

A book that every lady should study and every household possess. An intensely interesting chapter on girlhood. Education of women. A very practical chapter on general hygiene, including hygiene of the skin and hygiene of the digestive organs. Sympathetic articles on motherhood and the hygiene of childhood. Also hygiene of the respiratory organs, hygiene of the eye, hygiene of the ear, hygiene of the generative organs. Cloth, **75** cents ; paper, **50** cents.

---

*For sale by all booksellers, or sent postpaid on receipt of advertised price.*

# THE WERNER COMPANY, Publishers, - Akron, O.

# THE WERNER COMPANY'S PUBLICATIONS.

# THE WERNER COMPANY'S PUBLICATIONS.

## MAGNER'S STANDARD HORSE BOOK.

By D. MAGNER. The well-known authority on training, educating, taming and treating horses. The most complete work of the kind in existence ; strongly endorsed by leading horse experts everywhere. Large quarto volume ; 638 pages ; over one thousand illustrations. Half Russia binding. Price, $2.50.

## THE BIBLE FOR YOUNG PEOPLE.

In words of easy reading. The sweet stories of God's word. In the language of childhood. By the gifted author, JOSEPHINE POLLARD. Beautifully illustrated with nearly two hundred fifty striking original engravings and world-famous masterpieces of Sacred Art, and with magnificent colored plates. *The Bible For Young People* is complete in one sumptuous, massive, nearly square octavo volume, of over five hundred pages. Bound in extra cloth, ink and gold sides and back. $1.50.

## GLIMPSES OF THE WORLD.

Hundreds of full-page views. Portraying scenes all over the world. The views composing this superb volume are reproduced by the perfected half-tone process from photographs collected by the celebrated traveler and lecturer, JOHN L. STODDARD, by whom the pictures are described in graphic language. In Glimpses of the World is presented a grand panorama of England, Scotland, and Ireland, France, Germany, Russia, Austria, Turkey, Italy, Spain, Asia, Africa, and North and South America. Unquestionably the finest work of the kind ever printed. Buckram. Price, $4.50.

## THE WERNER POCKET ATLAS OF THE UNITED STATES.

A real pocket atlas 5x3½ inches, 96 pages, leatherette covers. Needed by every traveling man. Should be on every desk. Price, 10 cents.

## THE CAPITOL COOK BOOK.

448 pages, 8½x6 inches ; weight, 1½ pounds ; over 1,400 tested recipes by HUGO ZIEMAN, ex-steward of the White House, and the well-known expert, Mrs. F. L. GILLETTE. Illustrated. Price, 50 cents.

## THE WALDORF COOK BOOK.

By "OSCAR" of the Waldorf. The most thorough and complete treatise on Practical Cookery ever published. The author, OSCAR TSCHIRKY, Maitre d'Hotel, The Waldorf and Astoria, is acknowledged to be one of the foremost culinary authorities of the world. Elaborate directions are given for making ice creams, ices, pastries and tea and coffee. Selections may be made to gratify any taste. Original and varied recipes are given for making toothsome confections, preserves, jams, pickles and other condiments. Over 900 pages. Valuable information, indispensable to families, hotels, cafes and boarding houses. Wholesome, palatable, economic and systematic cooking. Everything used as food is fully considered. Nearly 4,000 recipes. The best and most comprehensive cook book compiled. Special features, such as suggestions with regard to the kitchen, menus, bills of fare, the seasons, market, etc., etc. Size, 8x10½ x 2¾ inches. Bound in one large octavo volume of over 900 pages in handsome oil cloth. Price, $2.50.

## THE STORY OF AMERICAN HEROISM.

As told by the Medal Winners and Roll of Honor men. A remarkable collection of thrilling, historical incidents of personal adventures during and after the great Civil War. Narratives by such heroes as Gen. LEW WALLACE, Gen. O. O. HOWARD, Gen. ALEX. WEBB, Gen. FITZHUGH LEE, Gen. WADE HAMPTON. A war gallery of noted men and events. A massive volume of over 700 pages, printed on fine calendered paper. Illustrated with three hundred original drawings of personal exploits. English cloth, emblematic design in gold and colors, $2.50.

*For sale by all booksellers, or sent postpaid on receipt of the advertised price.*

# THE WERNER COMPANY, Publishers, - Akron, O.